TEEN POP
BROADWAY COLLECTION
COMPILED BY MARIANN COOK

28 SONGS FROM 20 SHOWS

BILLY ELLIOT

ZOMBIE PROM

SPRING AWAKENING

BARE

13

REEFER MADNESS

CAPTAIN LOUIE

STARMITES

runaways

HOW TO EAT LIKE A CHILD

Piano/vocal arrangements by John Nicholas
("Sayonara" and "Waiting Waiting" arranged by John Forster)

Cherry Lane Music Company
Director of Publications/Project Editor: Mark Phillips

ISBN 978-1-60378-295-1

Visit our website at www.cherrylaneprint.com

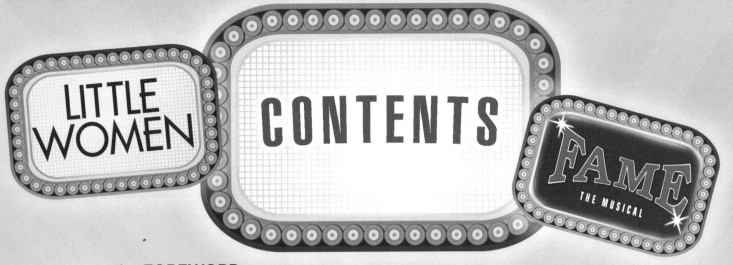

CONTENTS

FOREWORD

As a voice instructor of contemporary commercial music, I often teach workshops for young people who want to sing in Pop and Broadway styles. A frequent complaint I receive from parents and teachers is the lack of age-appropriate literature in these genres for young voices. Current vocal books for teens consist mostly of songs written for adults (the songs from *Wicked*, for example). In the studio, my Internet-savvy students constantly bring in songs they find on YouTube or discover in some obscure show. As I began to collect lists of these songs, the idea for this compilation came to mind.

The large majority of songs within, written by composers who have had successful Broadway shows, are often sung but have never been printed in Vocal Selection form. The age range varies from preteen to advanced teen; there are even a few for unchanged voice. It is my hope that this collection will provide teachers and performers with new age-appropriate show tunes for use in auditions and studio. If you would like more information on any of the shows from which these songs are taken, I have listed the contacts below. Enjoy!

—Mariann Cook
Professor of Musical Theatre Voice
Westminster College of the Arts at Rider University
mcook@rider.edu

BARE

Writers
Music: Damon Intrabartolo
Lyrics: Jon Hartmere
Book: Jon Hartmere and Damon Intrabartolo

First performance
Hudson Theatre, Los Angeles, October 2000
American Theatre of Actors, off-Broadway,
 April 2004

Licensing
Theatrical Rights Worldwide
866-378-975 (toll free)
www.theatricalrights.com
licensing@theatricalrights.com

BILLY ELLIOT

Writers
Music: Elton John
Book and Lyrics: Lee Hall

First performance
Broadway, 2009

Licensing
Not licensed at this time.

CALVIN BERGER

Writer
Music/Lyrics: Barry Wyner

First performance
George Street Playhouse, New Brunswick, NJ,
  February 19, 2010
Earlier versions were presented at Gloucester
  Stage (Gloucester, MA) and Barrington Stage
  (Pittsfield, MA).

Licensing
Tams-Witmark Music Library
800-221-7196
Tams-Witmark.com

CAPTAIN LOUIE

Writers
Music/Lyrics: Stephen Schwartz
Book: Anthony Stein

First performance
York Theatre (off-Broadway), 2005

Licensing
MTI–Music Theatre International
421 West 54th Street
New York, NY 10019
212-541-4684, 212-397-4684 (fax)
Licensing@MTIshows.com

CHILDREN'S LETTERS TO GOD

Writers
Music: David Evans
Lyrics: Douglas J. Cohen

First performance
Lamb's Theater, New York, June 19, 2004

Licensing
Samuel French, Inc.
212-206-8990, 866-598-8449 (toll free),
  212-206-1429 (fax)
Amateur/Non-Professional Musical Department:
  musicals@samuelfrench.com
Professional Leasing Department:
  professional@samuelfrench.com

DADDY LONG LEGS

Writers
Music/Lyrics: Paul Gordon
Book: John Caird

First performance
Rubicon Theatre, Ventura, CA, 2009

Licensing
See website, daddlylonglegsmusical.com,
  or Daddy Long Legs on Facebook

FAME (The Film)

Writer
Music/Lyrics: Michael Gore

Date released
1980

FLIGHT OF THE LAWNCHAIR MAN

Writers
Music/Lyrics/Concept: Robert Lindsey-Nassif
Book: Peter Ullian

First performance
Prince Music Theatre, Philadelphia,
  November 2000
Goodspeed Opera House, May, 2005

Licensing
Theatrical Rights Worldwide
866-378-975 (toll free)
www.theatricalrights.com
licensing@theatricalrights.com

FOOTLOOSE (The Musical)

Writers
Music: Tom Snow
Lyrics: Dean Pitchford
Book: Dean Pitchford and Walter Bobbie

First performance
Richard Rodgers Theatre, Broadway,
  October 22, 1998

Licensing
R&H Theatricals—Amateur Theatres
800-400-8160, 212-268-1245 (fax)
amtheatre@rnh.com
R&H Theatricals—Professional Theatres
212-541-6600, 568-6155 (fax)
protheatre@rnh.com

HOW TO EAT LIKE A CHILD

Writers
Music/Lyrics: John Forster
Book: Delia Ephron, John Forster, and Judith Kahan

First performance
Television special, 1980

Licensing
Samuel French, Inc.
212-206-8990, 866-598-8449 (toll free),
  212-206-1429 (fax)
Amateur/Non-Professional Musical Department:
  musicals@samuelfrench.com
Professional Leasing Department:
  professional@samuelfrench.com

LITTLE WOMEN

Writers
Music: Jason Howland
Lyrics: Mindi Jackson
Book: Allen Knee

First performance
Virginia Theatre, January 23, 2005

Licensing
MTI—Music Theatre International
421 West 54th Street
New York, NY 10019
212-541-4684, 212-397-4684 (fax)
Licensing@MTIshows.com

ON COMMON GROUND

Writer
Music/Lyrics: David Austin

First performance
University of Oklahoma, in conjunction with the
  Lyric Theatre of Oklahoma, July 1, 2009

Licensing
Abrams Artists
646-461-9383
peter.hagan@abramsartny.com

REEFER MADNESS

Writers
Music: Dan Studney
Book/Lyrics: Kevin Murphy

First performance
Off-Broadway, 2001; currently running
  off-Broadway

Licensing
R&H Theatricals—Amateur Theatres
800-400-8160, 212-268-1245 (fax)
amtheatre@rnh.com
R&H Theatricals—Professional Theatres
212-541-6600, 212-568-6155 (fax)
protheatre@rnh.com

ROALD DAHL'S WILLIE WONKA

Writers
Music/Lyrics: Leslie Bricusse and
  Anthony Newley

First performance
Kennedy Center, Washington, D.C.,
  November 2004

Licensing
MTI—Music Theatre International
421 West 54th Street
New York, NY 10019
212-541-4684, 212-397-4684 (fax)
Licensing@MTIshows.com

RUNAWAYS (The Musical)

Writer
Music/Lyrics: Elizabeth Swados

First performance
Broadway, May 13, 1978

Licensing
Samuel French, Inc.
212-206-8990, 866-598-8449 (toll free),
  212-206-1429 (fax)
Amateur/Non-Professional Musical Department:
  musicals@samuelfrench.com
Professional Leasing Department:
  professional@samuelfrench.com

SPRING AWAKENING

Writers
Music: Duncan Sheik
Book/Lyrics: Steven Sater

First performance
Broadway, December 10, 2005

Licensing
MTI—Music Theatre International
421 West 54th Street
New York, NY 10019
212-541-4684, 212-397-4684 (fax)
Licensing@MTIshows.com

STARMITES

Writers
Music/Lyrics: Barry Keating
Book: Stuart Ross

First performance
Broadway, April 27, 1989

Licensing
Samuel French, Inc.
212-206-8990, 866-598-8449 (toll free),
  212-206-1429 (fax)
Amateur/Non-Professional Musical Department:
  musicals@samuelfrench.com
Professional Leasing Department:
  professional@samuelfrench.co

SUMMER OF '42

Writers
Music/Lyrics: David Kirshenbaum
Book: Hunter Foster

First performance
Off-Broadway, December 2001

Licensing
Dramatists Play Service
212-683-8960
www.dramatists.com
postmaster@dramatists.com

13

Writers
Music/Lyrics: Jason Robert Brown
Book: Don Elish and Robert Horn

First performance
Mark Tauper Forum, Los Angeles, California,
  January 7, 2007

Licensing
MTI—Music Theatre International
421 West 54th Street
New York, NY 10019
212-541-4684, 212-397-4684 (fax)
Licensing@MTIshows.com

ZOMBIE PROM

Writers
Music: Dana P. Rowe
Lyrics: John Dempsey

First performance
Off-Broadway, April 9, 1996

Licensing
Samuel French, Inc.
212-206-8990, 866-598-8449 (toll free),
  212-206-1429 (fax)
Amateur/Non-Professional Musical Department:
  musicals@samuelfrench.com
Professional Leasing Department:
  professional@samuelfrench.com

All Grown Up

from the Off-Broadway Musical BARE

Lyrics by
Jon Hartmere

Music by
Damon Intrabartolo

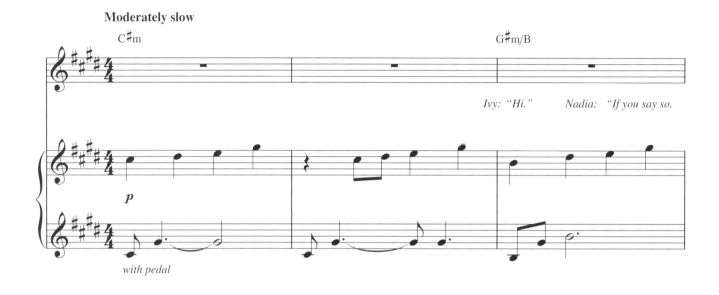

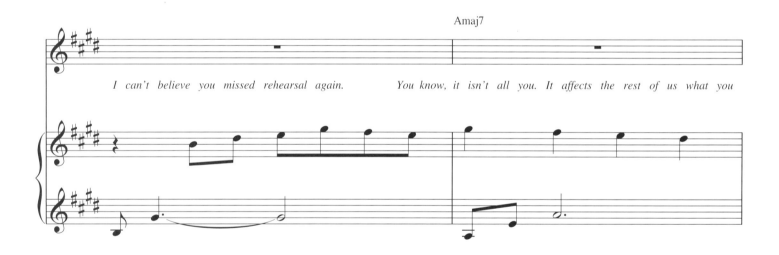

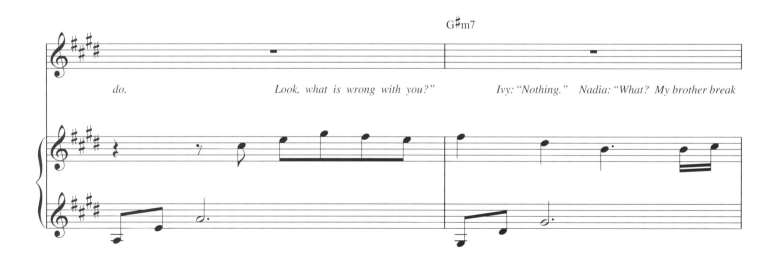

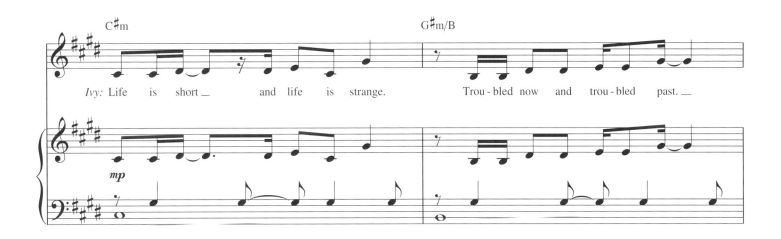

Feel it, how it grows in - side me. Swirl - ing ball of an - guished cries,

haunt - ed, daunt - ed, so un - want - ed. Feel its an - ger in ___ me rise.

Dream a dream ___ then dash an - oth - er. Life is there to in - ter - rupt. ___

Some - one out ___ there call my moth - er. Look at me, Mom, I'm all grown up.

Lyrics:

All those years she scrimped and saved, __ and now, of course, it comes to this. __ If

on - ly I - vy had be - haved __ or learned to stop __ at just a kiss. __ It

hits me, par - a - lyz - ing shud - der. Face the mu - sic, take a bow.

Tempo I

Lit - tle lies and __ big de - ci - sions, who to __ tell and where to go? __

Fol - low some - one else - 's vi - sion or trust my own __ 'cause I don't know. __ Am

I sup - posed to love this child? __ Is it just that __ sim - ple then?

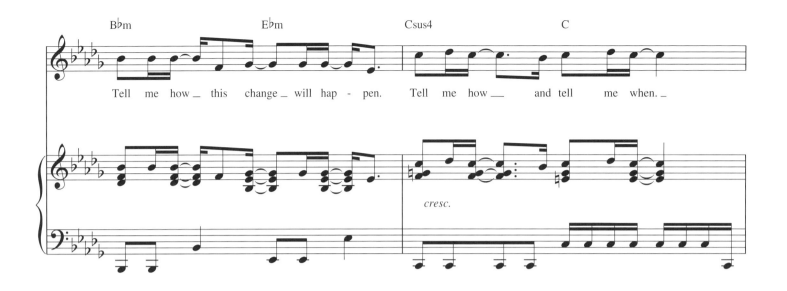

Tell me how __ this change __ will hap - pen. Tell me how __ and tell me when. __

Tell me how and tell me when. __ Dream a dream then __ dash an - oth - er.

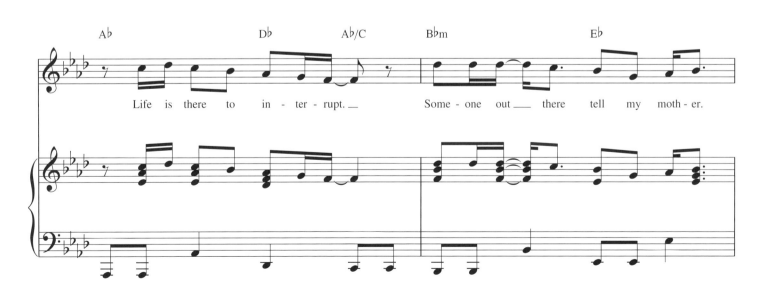

Life is there to in - ter - rupt. __ Some - one out __ there tell my moth - er.

Beauty Within

from the Broadway Musical STARMITES

Words and Music by
Barry Keating

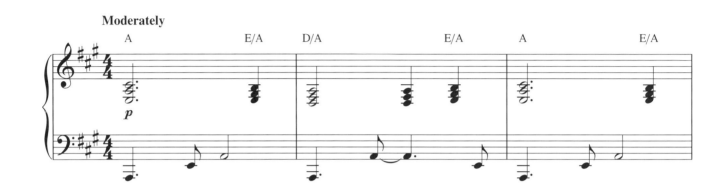

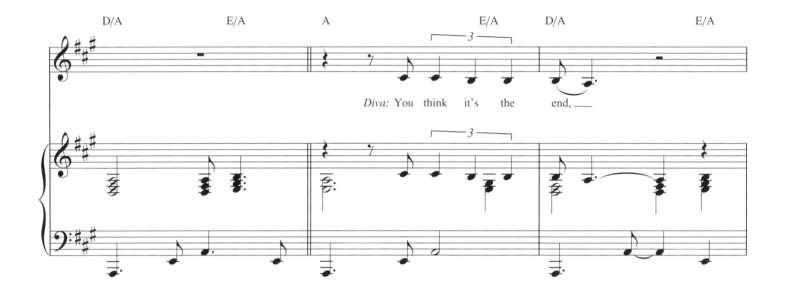

Diva: You think it's the end, ___

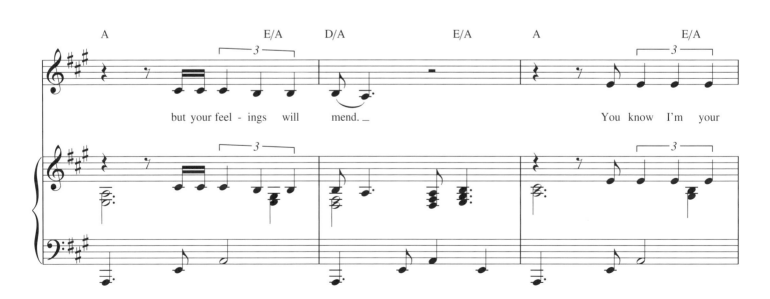

but your feel - ings will mend. __ You know I'm your

eye of the be - hold - er. What good is that if they nev - er will o - pen their eyes? _____

_____ You tell me: "Chin up, girl. Be bold - er." I could o - pen my heart. _____ But I'm a -

fraid if I start, _____ it might just rip me a - part _____ if I found out you've been tell - ing me

lies. _____

20

*Bizarbara sings top note.

There's no need to hide. You fi-n'lly let it all show.
There's no need to hide.

You fi-n'lly let it be-gin. You fi-n'lly found the beau-ty with-in

and sent it shin-ing through. Ah.
...and sent it shin-ing through. Ah.

Easy to Say

from the Off-Broadway Musical ZOMBIE PROM

Lyrics by
John Dempsey

Music by
Dana Rowe

Moderately

Find - ing the slope __ of *x* and *y*, __ and Jon - ny's there. __

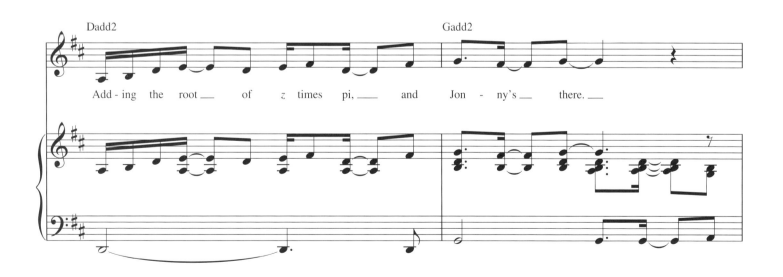

Add - ing the root __ of *z* times pi, __ and Jon - ny's __ there. __

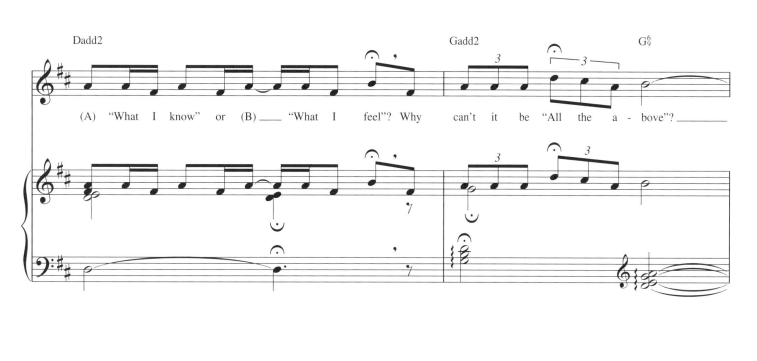

(A) "What I know" or (B) ___ "What I feel"? Why can't it be "All the a - bove"? ___

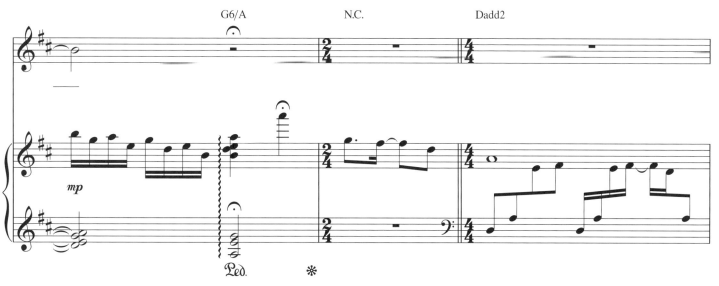

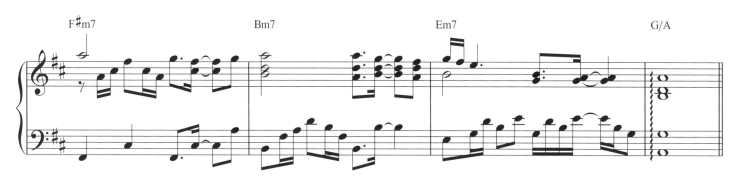

laid his bod - y six feet un - der, but e - ven death can't steal the thun - der of

teen - ag - ers in love. _____

Eas - y ____ to

Electricity

from the Broadway Musical BILLY ELLIOT

Lyrics by
Lee Hall

Music by
Elton John

Moderately slow

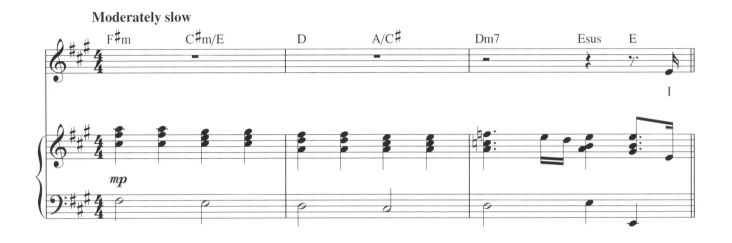

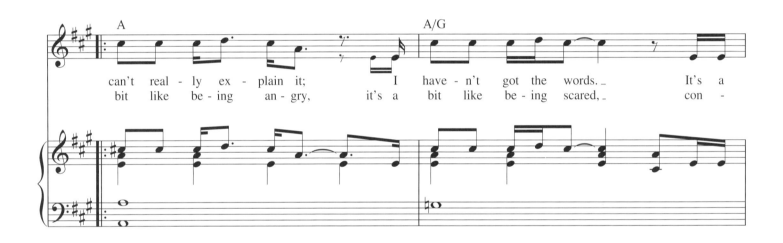

can't real - ly ex - plain it;   I have - n't got the words. _ It's a
bit like be - ing an - gry,   it's a bit like be - ing scared, _ con -

feel - ing that you can't con - trol. ____ I sup -
fused and all mixed up, and mad as hell. ____ It's ___

feel a change / feel it move me, like a fire___ deep in - side, ___ / like a burn - ing deep in - side, ___

some - thing burst - ing me wide o - pen, im - pos - si - ble ___ to hide. ___ And

sud - den - ly ___ I'm fly - ing, fly - ing like a bird, ___ like e - lec -

tric - i - ty. E - lec - tric - i - ty sparks in -

How Can I Say Good-bye

from the Off-Broadway Musical ZOMBIE PROM

Lyrics by
John Dempsey

Music by
Dana Rowe

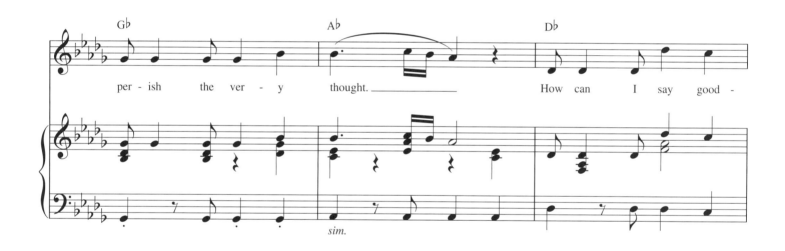

I Think I Like Her

from the Off-Broadway Musical SUMMER OF '42

Words and Music by
David Kirshenbaum

I think I like her. I think she's one of a kind, __ like Gret-a
cof-fee; I nev-er tried it be-fore. __ It near-ly

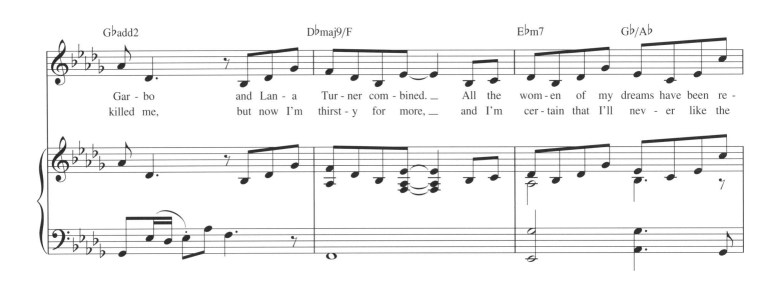

Gar-bo and Lan-a Tur-ner com-bined. __ All the wom-en of my dreams have been re-
killed me, but now I'm thirst-y for more, __ and I'm cer-tain that I'll nev-er like the

I Want to Fly

from the Off-Broadway Musical FLIGHT OF THE LAWNCHAIR MAN

Words and Music by
Robert Lindsey-Nassif

I've Got a Golden Ticket

from the Musical ROALD DAHL'S WILLY WONKA

Words and Music by
Leslie Bricusse and Anthony Newley

I've got a gold-en twin-kle in my eye!_____
I've got a gold-en sun up in my sky!_____

I nev-er thought I'd see the day when I would face the world and say, "Good-

morn - ing, _____ Look at the sun!"_____

It Just Wasn't Meant to Happen

from the Musical CALVIN BERGER

Words and Music by
Barry Wyner

just not ___ what she is af - ter; ___

just not ___ her cup of tea. _____ I'm

just gon - na have to move on; ___

just have ___ to let it go. It would have ___ been

Let's Hear It for the Boy

from the Broadway Musical FOOTLOOSE

Words by
Dean Pitchford

Music by
Tom Snow

Life So Far

from the Musical ON COMMON GROUND

Words and Music by
David Austin

Like Other Girls

from the Musical DADDY LONG LEGS

Words and Music by
Paul Gordon

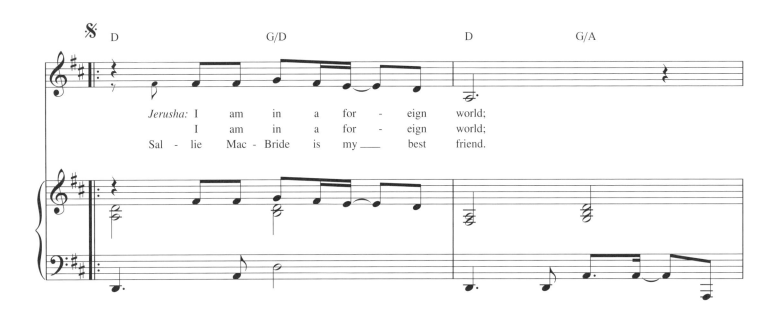

Jerusha: I am in a for - eign world;
I am in a for - eign world;
Sal - lie Mac - Bride is my ___ best friend.

they speak a lan - guage of ___ their ___ own. ___
I am dif - f'rent; I ___ am ___ strange. ___
I told her that ___ my folks ___ had ___ died ___

*Recorded a half step lower.

Em   G/D   A/C♯   A

No - bod - y knows where I _____ have   come ___ from, Dad - dy. ___
I   know that I should try ___ to   fit _____ in some - how, _
'cause   I can't tell her where _ I   come ___ from, Dad - dy. ___

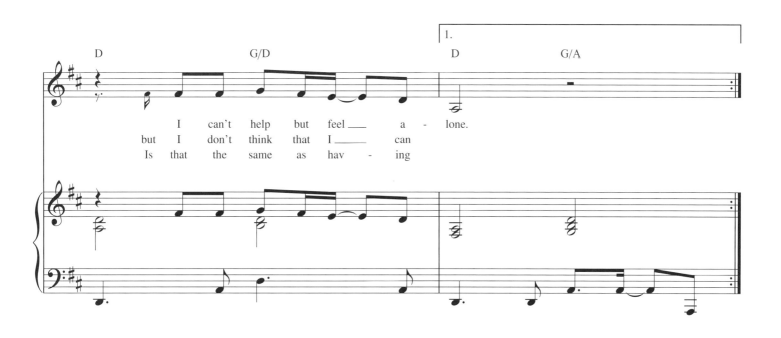

D   G/D   D   G/A

1.

I can't help but feel ___ a - lone.
but I don't think that I _____ can
Is that the same as hav - ing

2.

D   G/D   A

change.
lied?   And I know you won't be - lieve _
                        For I have shut out the re - mem-

To Coda ⊕

88

but I don't think that I ___ can ___ change.
but I don't think that I ___ can ___ change.

And I know you won't be-lieve ___ it, but I just wan-na be ___
I just wan-na be... ___

___ like oth-er girls; ___ get all ___ dressed up ___ like oth-er girls; be-come a
___ Get all ___ dressed up. ___

sci - en - tist, a mo-tor-ist, ___ a suf-fra-gette, ___ a Meth-od-ist, ___ a
Sci - en - tist, a Meth - od-ist, ___ a

Lullaby from Baby to Baby

from the Broadway Musical RUNAWAYS

Words and Music by
Elizabeth Swados

mor - row will be a dif - f'rent world ___ than the way it was ___ to - day. ___

A wom - an gets a job in

New York Cit - y, ___

(Got - ta get a - way, got - ta get a - way now.)

for - gets she was a moth - er

and a wife, ___

(Got - ta get a - way, got - ta get a - way now.)

finds her - self a nice a - part -

ment and makes up for the last thir-ty-five years of her life. _____ Be - cause _____ a
(Of her life.)

ma - ma's got to run _____ from dad - dy. A ma - ma's got to

run _____ from child. _____ To - mor-row will be a dif - f'rent world, _____

lone - li - er _____ and wild. _____

(Ah, ah, ee ee. Ah, ah, ee ee. Ah, ah, ee ee. Ah, ah, ee ee.)

Thou-sands of cars go buzz-ing to and fro. ___ Air-planes and trains go

shoot-ing by. ___ Ev-'ry-bod-y goes from A ___ to B, ___ and

no-bod-y does ___ know why ___ be-cause ___ the world is full of
(Be-cause.)

peo - ple run - nin'. The world is made of run - a - ways.___ To-
(Run - nin'.)   (Run - a - ways.)

mor - row you'll be a dif - f'rent child ___ than the one you are ___ to - day. ___

(Ah,   ah,   ee   ee.

Ah,   ah,   ee   ee.   Ah,   ah,   ee   ee.   Ah,   ah,   ee   ee.)

Mama Who Bore Me
from the Broadway Musical SPRING AWAKENING

Lyrics by
Steven Sater

Music by
Duncan Sheik

No sleep _ in Heav-en or Beth - le-hem. _ Some pray that _ one day _ Christ _

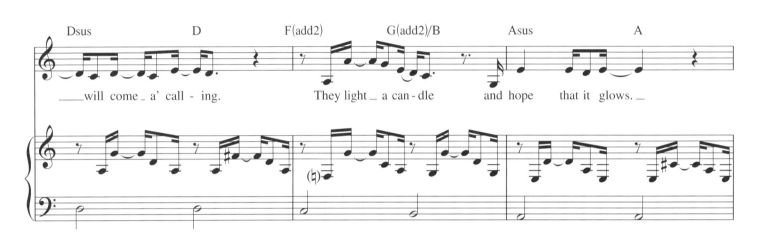

_ will come _ a' call - ing. They light _ a can - dle and hope that it glows. _

And some _ just lie _ there, cry - ing for him to come _ and find _ them. But

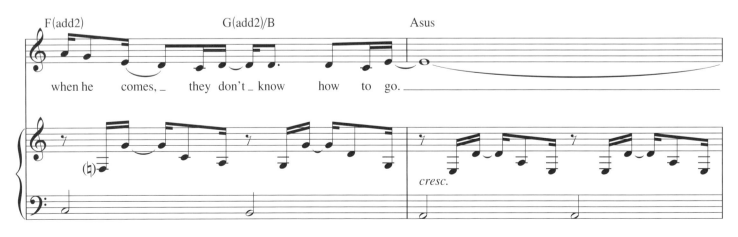

when he comes, _ they don't _ know how to go. _

cresc.

New Kid in the Neighborhood

from the Off-Broadway Musical CAPTAIN LOUIE

Music and Lyrics by
Stephen Schwartz

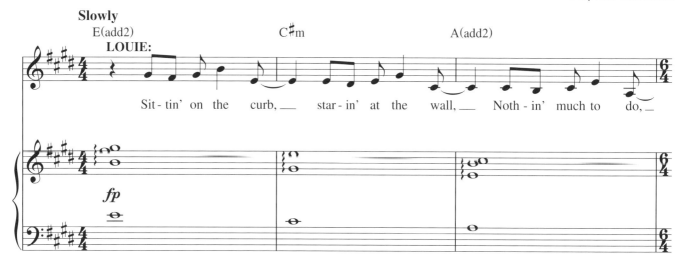

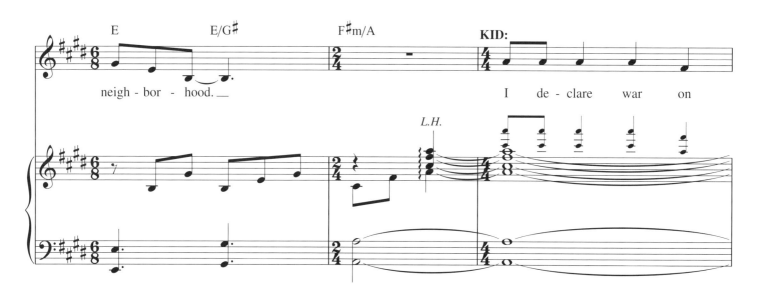

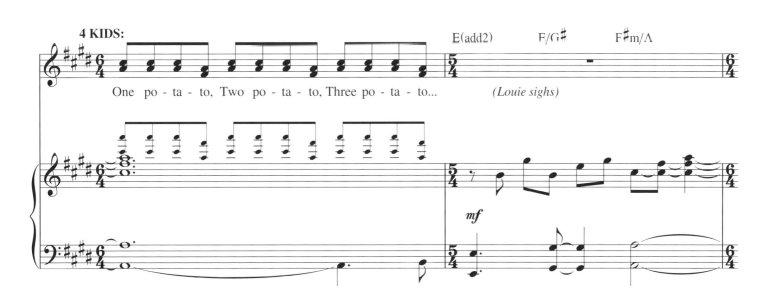

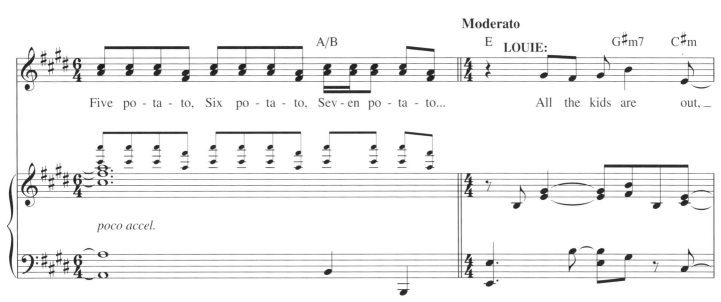

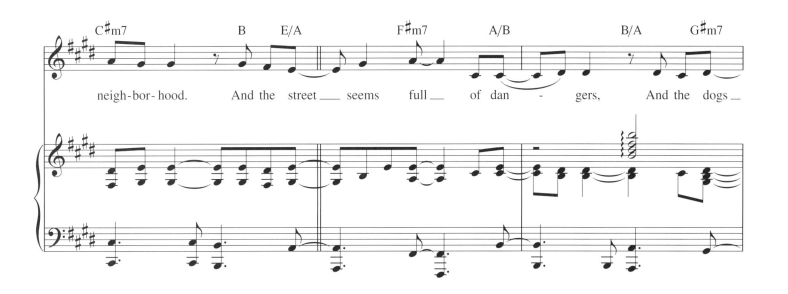

neigh-bor-hood. And the street ___ seems full ___ of dan - gers, And the dogs ___

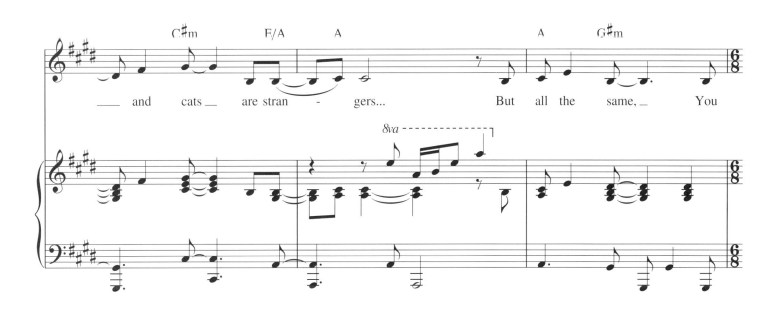

___ and cats ___ are stran - gers... But all the same, ___ You

wish you could run and join that game. ___

But they don't know your name, __ you don't know the score, __ All you know is

you're __ the new kid __ in a new neigh - bor -

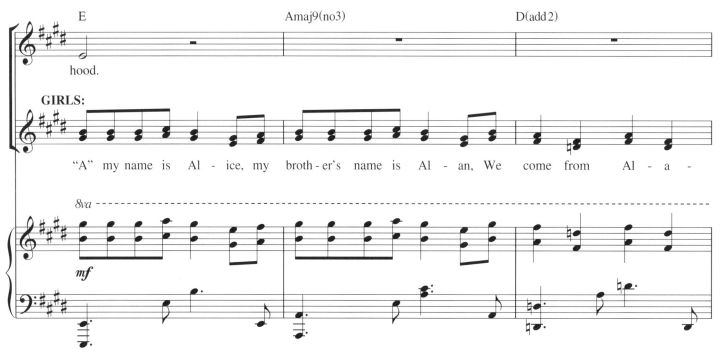

hood.

GIRLS:

"A" my name is Al - ice, my broth - er's name is Al - an, We come from Al - a -

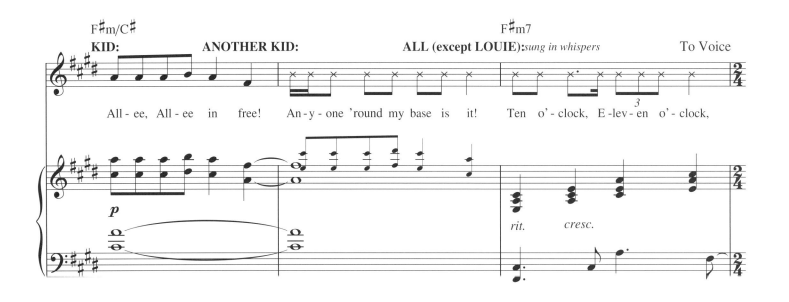

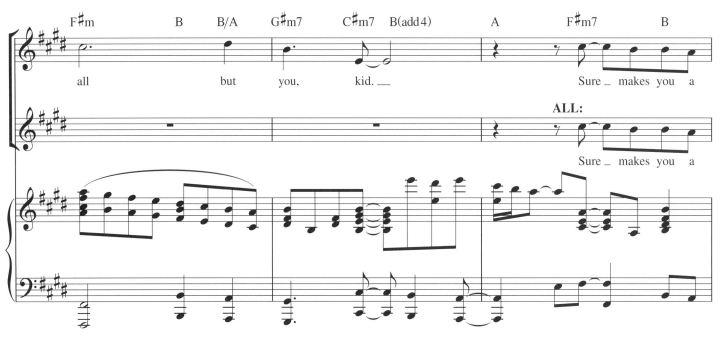

Out Here on My Own

from FAME

Words by
Lesley Gore

Music by
Michael Gore

Moderate Ballad

Some-times I won-der where I've been, who I am.

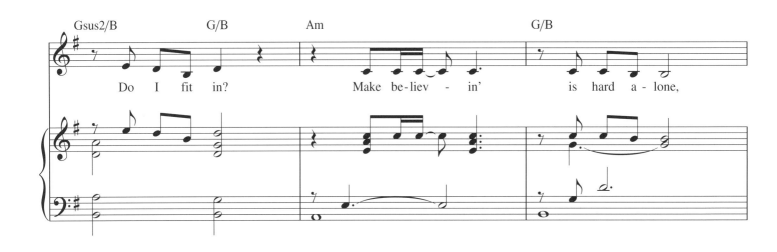

Do I fit in? Make be-liev-in' is hard a-lone,

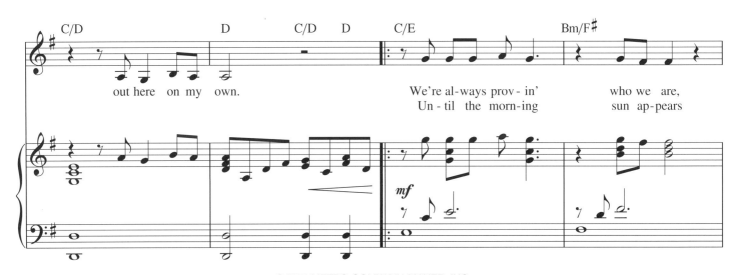

out here on my own.

We're al-ways prov-in' who we are,
Un-til the morn-ing sun ap-pears

Portrait of a Girl

from the Off-Broadway Musical BARE

Lyrics by
Jon Hartmere

Music by
Damon Intrabartolo

Moderately fast

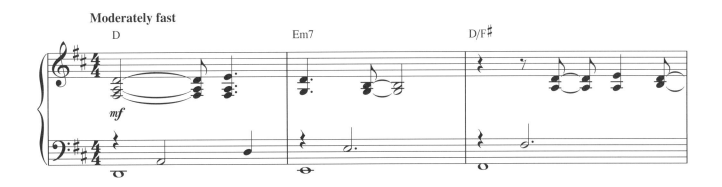

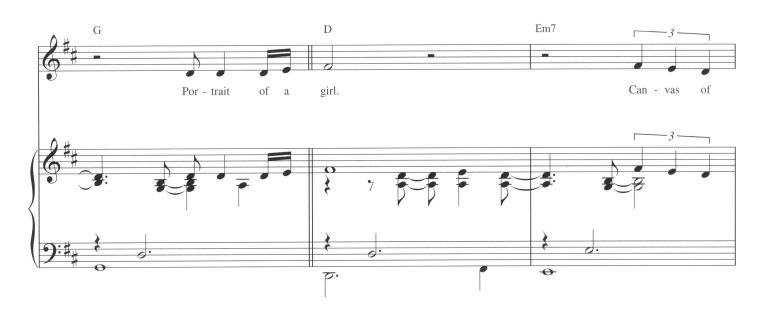

Por - trait of a girl. Can - vas of

ag - es. The stage is hers, de - mure in prac -

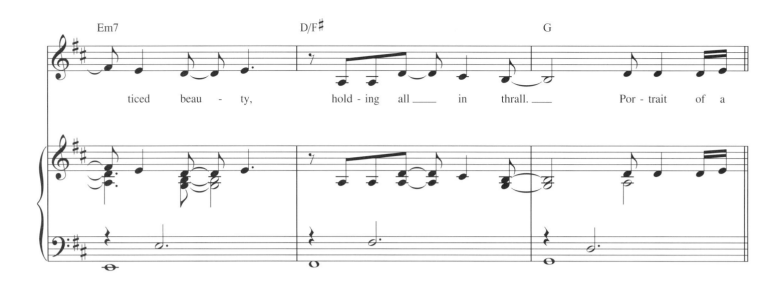

ticed beau - ty, hold - ing all ___ in thrall. ___ Por - trait of a

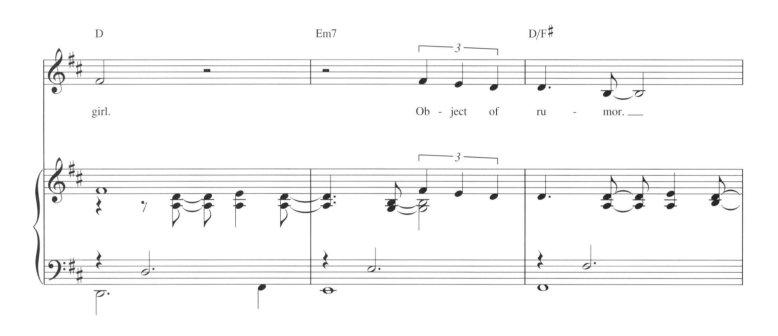

girl. Ob - ject of ru - mor. ___

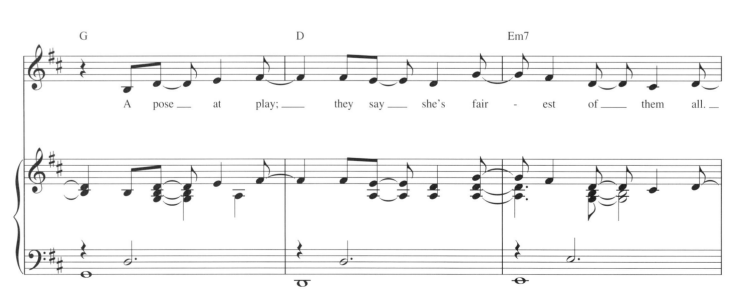

A pose ___ at play; ___ they say ___ she's fair - est of ___ them all.

Paint __ her in; __ one col-or ends __ and one __ be - gins. __

__ Brush a - way what's stray; __ add a fin - ish-ing touch. __ The rap - ture cold __

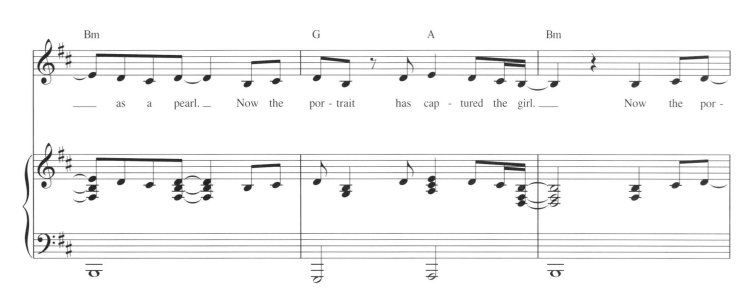

__ as a pearl. __ Now the por - trait has cap - tured the girl. __ Now the por -

120

Role of a Lifetime

from the Off-Broadway Musical BARE

Lyrics by
Jon Hartmere

Music by
Damon Intrabartolo

hop-ing that the house is not brought down. The

role of a life-time, it's liv-ing a fan-ta-sy, a

dra-ma that you strug-gle to e-rase.

Thoughts bat-tle words o-ver deeds, a war with such ca-sual-ties, all

hop - ing that one _ day when _ you wake, those _ feel - ings won't be _

_ there.

So con - fused _ be - cause _ I feel com - plete with him. _ When

we're a - lone, _ it all _ some - how _ makes sense.

Look in - to ___ his eyes ___ for some com - pro - mise; re - mem - ber the word "for - get" ___ and

try to bur - y some - thing so ___ in - tense. ___

You learn to play the straight man; your

lines be - come rou - tine, nev - er ___ real - ly ___

Romeo and Juliet

from the Off-Broadway Musical REEFER MADNESS

Words and Music by
Dan Studney and Kevin Murphy

Moderately fast

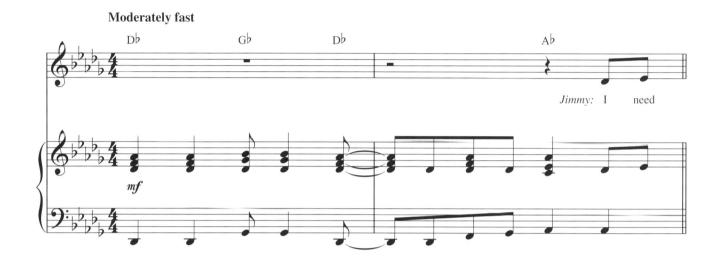

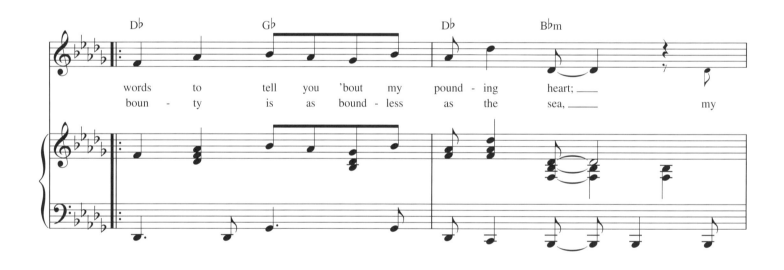

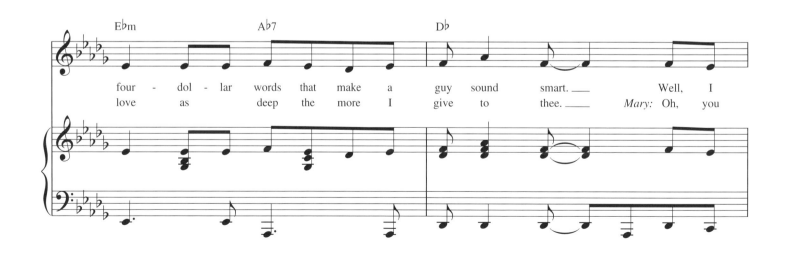

guess that's why they in - vent - ed Shake - speare.
sound so dream - y when you talk like Shake - speare. *Both:* A

His ar - tic - u - la - tions of a lov - er's pal - pi - ta - tions are so keen.
big vo - cab - u - lar - y should be cus - tom - ar - y when you fall in

My ___ love. ___ *Jimmy:* La la

la la la la. You're a snow - y dove. ___ *Mary:* La la la, pro - di - gious

*Jimmy sings top notes.

read the end - ing. I can't ei - ther! But I'm sure it turns out real swell. I bet

Juliet:

Ro - me - o mar - ries his Ju - li - et.

Jimmy: They have a ba - by and make lots of friends. *Juliet:* *Both:* That's

prob - 'ly the way the play ends.

Saturday Alone

from the Musical CALVIN BERGER

Words and Music by
Barry Wyner

Sat - ur - day _ a - lone, _ and I can't stop _ think - ing _
Sat - ur - day _ a - lone _ with - out a friend or _ boy - friend, _

I should be out there hav - ing fun.
which I ad - mit gets pret - ty hard.

136

Sayonara

from the Musical HOW TO EAT LIKE A CHILD

Words and Music by
John Forster

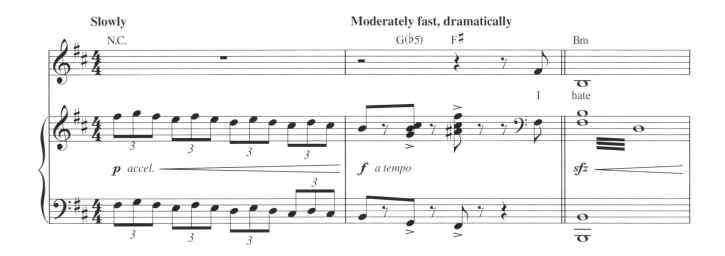

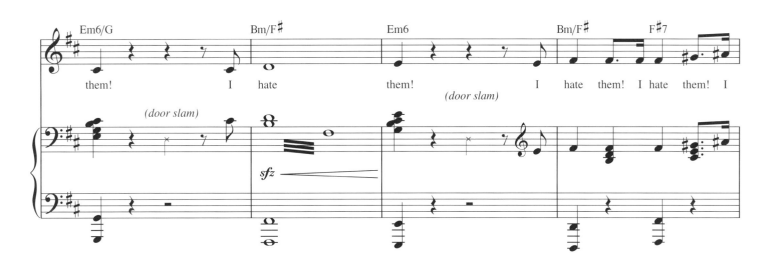

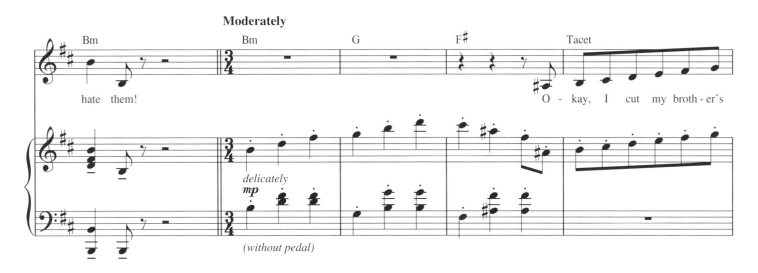

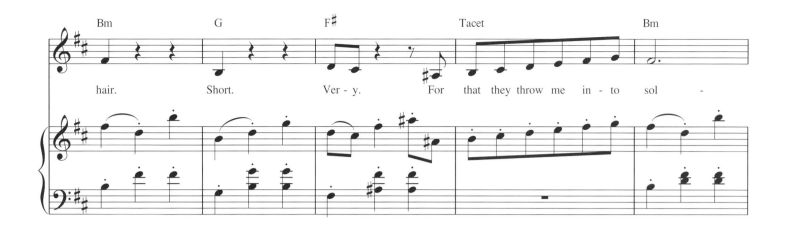

hair. Short. Ver - y. For that they throw me in - to sol -

i - tar - y with noth - ing up here but my pri - vate

ster - e - o me - di - a cen - ter to keep me dis - tract - ed. Well,

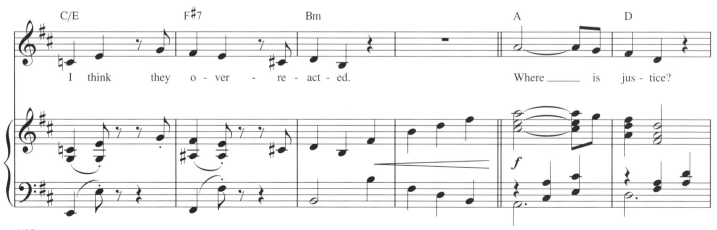

I think they o - ver - re - act - ed. Where ____ is jus - tice?

four times a year I'll come by late at night to col-lect it. Sa - yo - na - ra. Good - bye __ for good. Don't _____ feel guilt - y, e - ven though you should. Tell Grand-ma to think of me now and then. Tell Girl Scouts that I've re - lo - cat - ed. Tell

144

The Secret of Happiness

from the Musical DADDY LONG LEGS

Words and Music by
Paul Gordon

Moderately, in 4

I've dis-cov — ered the se-cret of hap-pi-ness __ is

learn - ing __ how to glide.

I've just dis - covered the se-cret of hap-pi-ness __ is

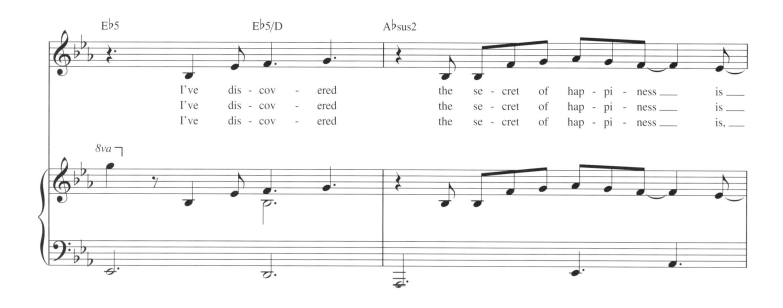

I've dis - cov - ered the se - cret of hap - pi - ness ___ is ___
I've dis - cov - ered the se - cret of hap - pi - ness ___ is ___
I've dis - cov - ered the se - cret of hap - pi - ness ___ is,

___ not ___ to run ___ too fast. _____
___ all ___ il - lu - sions fade. _____
___ though we can run ___ that hill, _____

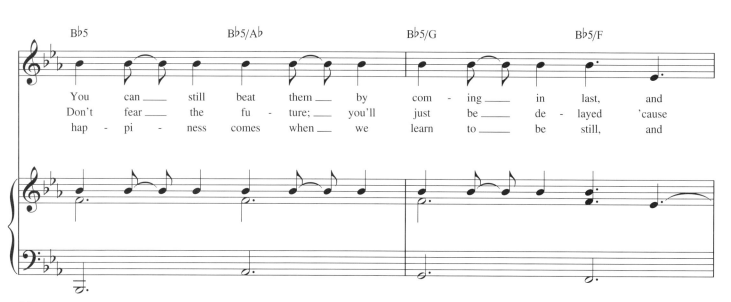

You can ___ still beat them ___ by com - ing ___ in last, and
Don't fear ___ the fu - ture; ___ you'll just be ___ de - layed 'cause
hap - pi - ness comes when ___ we learn to ___ be still, and

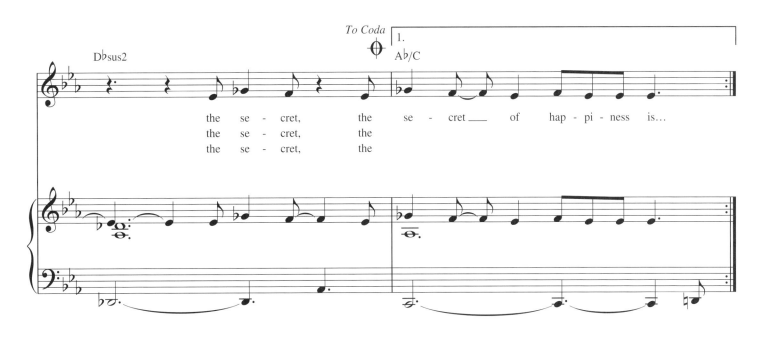

the se - cret, the se - cret___ of hap - pi - ness is...
the se - cret, the
the se - cret, the

se - cret___ of hap - pi - ness is _____ liv - ing in ___ the now.

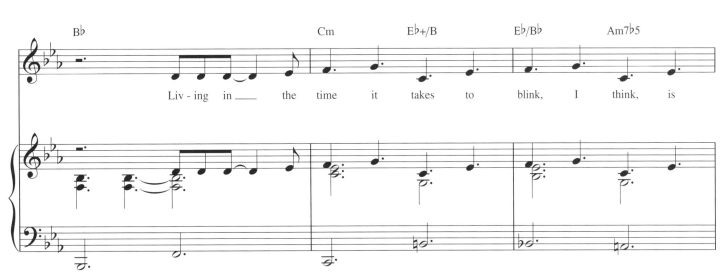

Liv - ing in ___ the time it takes to blink, I think, is

Silly Old Hat

from the Off-Broadway Musical CHILDREN'S LETTERS TO GOD

Words by
Douglas J. Cohen

Music by
David Evans

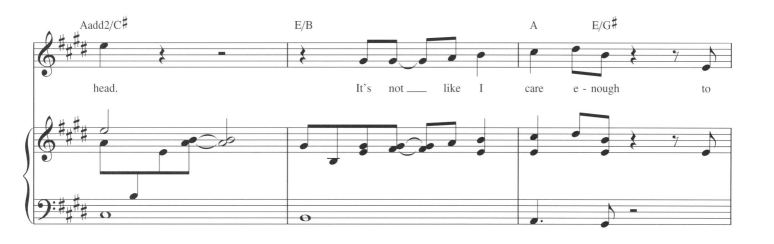

prob - lems ___ with math or get read - y for bed.

I've got this sil - ly old

hat that I wear on my head. _____

Six Hours as a Princess

from the Off-Broadway Musical CHILDREN'S LETTERS TO GOD

Words by
Douglas J. Cohen

Music by
David Evans

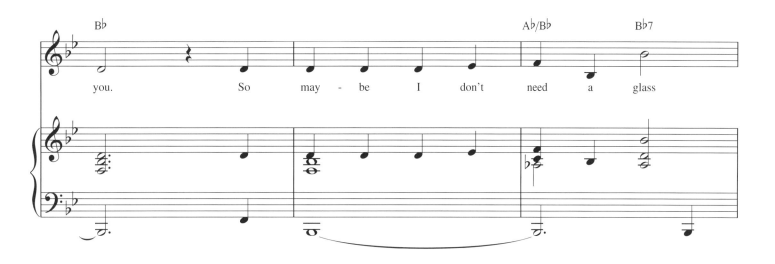

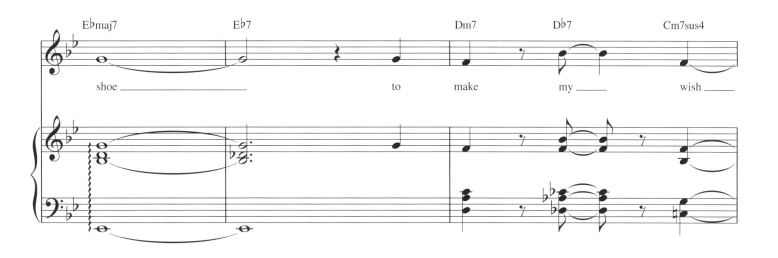

think that I'm al - lowed? Just one ho - ur as a

prin - cess. *O - K, ten min - utes!* I'm not proud. ___ And the

night will be filled ___ with stars, ___ and he'll be hold - ing my hand. ___

___ And Brett will say ___ he cares ___ for me 'cause

Some Things Are Meant to Be

from the Broadway Musical LITTLE WOMEN

Lyrics by
Mindi Dickstein

Music by
Jason Howland

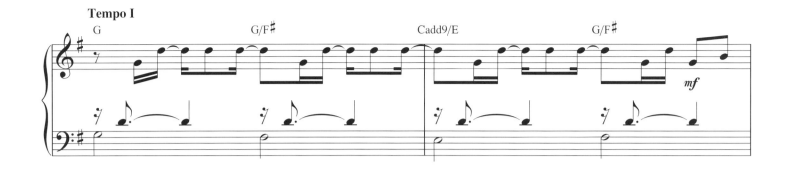

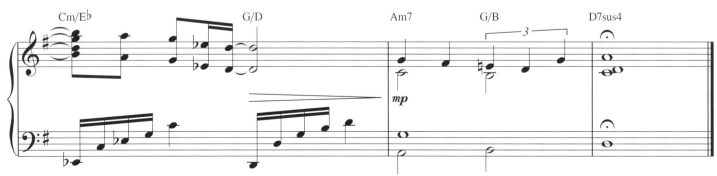

Superhero Girl

from the Broadway Musical STARMITES

Words and Music by
Barry Keating

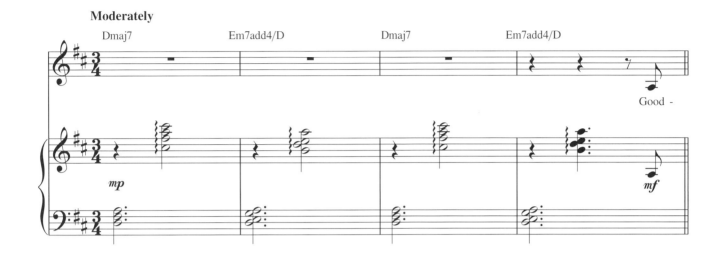

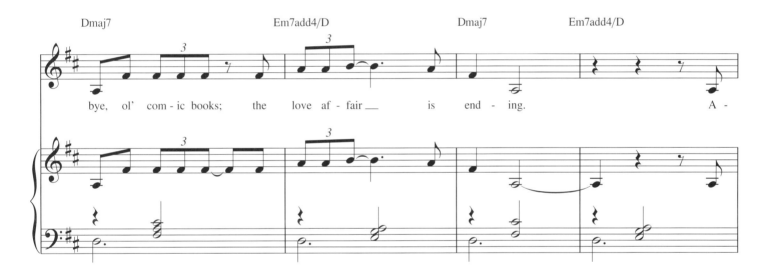

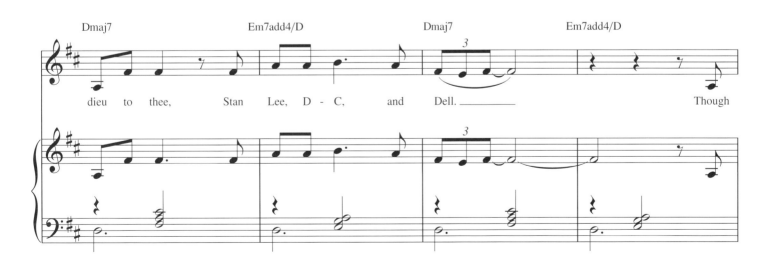

like in the com - ics, like in the mov - ies.

Oh, _____ some day I'll be a

su - per - he - ro girl, _____ faith - ful and force - ful and e -

ter - nal - ly true. I'll crush ev - 'ry en - e - my of the red, white, and blue; de -

fend my fel - low men and my fel - low wom - en, too.

That's what I'm gon - na do. But, oh, _____

_____ it's tough to be a su - per - he - ro girl _____

'cause no one knows it. I'm much too shy to show it.

Slower

(Rap:) I'll swoop down on the scene look-in' so cra-zy cool. ___ So fierce and choice and fly, the boys can't help but drool. ___ The lord of e-vil thinks that he can rule big time, ___ but I'll meg-a-blast that bust-a, mess him up real fine. ___

Waiting Waiting

from the Musical HOW TO EAT LIKE A CHILD

Words and Music by
John Forster

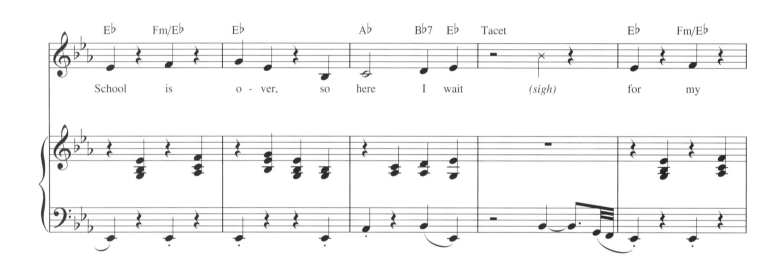

Slightly faster (♩♩ = ♩♩)

gone. Noth-ing makes ya thirst-i-er than wait - ing, wait - ing.

May-be I should have pitched a tent. Pret-ty soon I'll have pneu-mo-nia or an

ac-ci-dent. What if she clean for-got she

said half past two, and nev-er showed? What if a li-on that es-

What It Means to Be a Friend

from the Broadway Musical 13

Music and Lyrics by
Jason Robert Brown

Rock Ballad, rhythmically strong

what it means ___ to be ___ a friend. ___

friend won't smoke when she's in your room ___ Or laugh at the po - ems you write.

friend won't go and start kiss-ing your broth-er the min-ute that you're ___ out of sight. ___

188

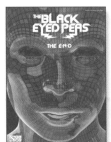

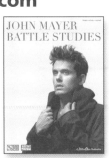